In your hands, more than 100 quotes about
life and for life.
Enjoy it !
Repeat each one several times, and think
over.
Reflect and enjoy your time with the cream of
the experiences of others.

"Life is like riding a bicycle. To keep your balance, you must keep moving."
— Albert Einstein

"The way I see it, if you want the rainbow, you gotta put up with the rain." —**Dolly Parton**

"Get busy living or get busy dying."
— Stephen King

"The purpose of our lives is
to be happy."
— Dalai Lama

"Never let the fear of striking out keep you from playing the game."– Babe Ruth

"Your time is limited, so don't waste it living someone else's life. Don't be trapped by dogma – which is living with the results of other people's thinking." – **Steve Jobs**

"Many of life's failures are people who did not realize how close they were to success when they gave up."
– Thomas A. Edison

"Money and success don't change people; they merely amplify what is already there."
— Will Smith

"If you want to live a happy life, tie it to a goal, not to people or things."
– Albert Einstein

"The big lesson in life, baby, is never
be scared of anyone or anything."
– Frank Sinatra

"Not how long, but how well you have lived is the main thing."
— Seneca

“In order to write about life first you must live it.– Ernest Hemingway

"If life were predictable it would cease to be life, and be without flavor."
– Eleanor Roosevelt

"Life is not a problem to be solved, but a reality to be experienced."
– Soren Kierkegaard

"Watch your thoughts; they become words. Watch your words, they become actions. Watch your actions; they become habits. Watch your habits, they become character. Watch your character; it becomes your destiny."
— Lao-Tze

"Sing like no one's listening, love like you've never been hurt, dance like nobody's watching, and live like it's heaven on earth."

– (Attributed to various sources)

"Curiosity about life in all of its aspects, I think, is still the secret of great creative people."
– Leo Burnett

"The unexamined life is not worth living."
— Socrates

"Turn your wounds
into wisdom."
— Oprah Winfrey

"Do all the good you can, for all the people you can, in all the ways you can, as long as you can."
— Hillary Clinton

"You only live once, but if you do it right, once is enough."
— Mae West

"Don't settle for what life gives you; make life better and build something."
— Ashton Kutcher

"Everybody wants to be famous, but nobody wants to do the work. I live by that. You grind hard so you can play hard. At the end of the day, you put all the work in, and eventually it'll pay off. It could be in a year, it could be in 30 years. Eventually, your hard work will pay off."
— Kevin Hart

"Everything negative pressure, challenges is all an opportunity for me to rise."
— Kobe Bryant

"I like criticism. It makes you strong."
— LeBron James

"You never really
learn much from
hearing yourself
speak."
— George Clooney

"Life imposes things on you that you can't control, but you still have the choice of how you're going to live through this."
— Celine Dion

"Life is never easy.
There is work to be
done and obligations
to be met obligations
to truth, to justice,
and to liberty."
— John F. Kennedy

"Live for each second
without hesitation."

— Elton John

"Life is what happens when you're busy making other plans."
— John Lennon

"Life is really simple, but men insist on making it complicated."

— Confucius

"Life is a succession of lessons which must be lived to be understood."
— Helen Keller

"Your work is going to fill a large part of your life, and the only way to be truly satisfied is to do what you believe is great work. And the only way to do great work is to love what you do. If you haven't found it yet, keep looking. Don't settle. As with all matters of the heart, you'll know when you find it."

— Steve Jobs

"My mama always said, life is like a box of chocolates. You never know what you're gonna get."
— Forrest Gump

"When we do the best we can, we never know what miracle is wrought in our life or the life of another."
— Helen Keller

"The healthiest response to life is joy."
—Deepak Chopra

"Life is like a coin. You can spend it any way you wish, but you only spend it once."
—Lillian Dickson

"The best portion of a good man's life is his little nameless, unencumbered acts of kindness and of love."
— **Wordsworth**

"In three words I can sum up everything I've learned about life: It goes on."
— Robert Frost

"Life is ten percent what happens to you and ninety percent how you respond to it."
— Charles Swindoll

"Keep calm and carry on."

— Winston Churchill

"Maybe that's what life is... a wink of the eye and winking stars."

— Jack Kerouac

"Life is a flower of which love is the honey."
— Victor Hugo

"Keep smiling, because life is a beautiful thing and there's so much to smile about."
—Marilyn Monroe

"Health is the greatest gift, contentment the greatest wealth, faithfulness the best relationship."

— Buddha

"You have brains in your head. You have feet in your shoes. You can steer yourself any direction you choose."

— Dr. Seuss

"Good friends, good books, and a sleepy conscience: this is the ideal life."
— Mark Twain

"Life would be tragic if it weren't funny." — Stephen Hawking

"Live in the sunshine, swim the sea, drink the wild air."

—Ralph Waldo Emerson

"The greatest pleasure of life
is love."

— Euripides

"Life is what we make it, always has been, always will be."

— Grandma Moses

"Life's tragedy is that we get old too soon and wise too late."

— Benjamin Franklin

"Life is about making an impact, not making an income."

— Kevin Kruse

"I've missed more than 9000 shots in my career. I've lost almost 300 games. 26 times I've been trusted to take the game winning shot and missed. I've failed over and over and over again in my life. And that is why I succeed."

– Michael Jordan

"Every strike brings me closer to the next home run."
– Babe Ruth

"The two most important days in your life are the day you are born and the day you find out why."

– Mark Twain

"Life shrinks or expands in proportion to one's courage."

– Anais Nin

"When I was 5 years old, my mother always told me that happiness was the key to life. When I went to school, they asked me what I wanted to be when I grew up. I wrote down 'happy'. They told me I didn't understand the assignment, and I told them they didn't understand life."

– John Lennon

"Too many of us are not living   our   dreams because we are living our fears." – Les Brown

"I believe every human has a finite number of heartbeats. I don't intend to waste any of mine."

—Neil Armstrong

"Live as if you were to die tomorrow. Learn as if you were to live forever."

—Mahatma Gandhi

"If you live long enough, you'll make mistakes. But if you learn from them, you'll be a better person."

—Bill Clinton

"Life is short, and it is here to be lived."

—Kate Winslet

"The longer I live, the more beautiful life becomes."

—Frank Lloyd Wright

"Every moment is a fresh beginning."

—T.S. Eliot

"When you cease to
dream you cease to live."

—Malcolm Forbes

"If you spend your whole life waiting for the storm, you'll never enjoy the sunshine."

—Morris West

"Don't cry because it's over, smile because it happened." —Dr. Seuss

"If you can do what you do best and be happy, you're further along in life than most people."

—Leonardo DiCaprio

"We should remember that just as a positive outlook on life can promote good health, so can everyday acts of kindness."

—Hillary Clinton

"It is our choices that show what we truly are, far more than our abilities."

—J. K. Rowling

"If you're not stubborn, you'll give up on experiments too soon. And if you're not flexible, you'll pound your head against the wall and you won't see a different solution to a problem you're trying to solve."
—Jeff Bezos

I guess it comes down to a simple choice, really. Get busy living or get busy dying."

—Shawshank Redemption

"The best way to predict your future is to create it."
— Abraham Lincoln

"You must expect great things of yourself before you can do them."

—Michael Jordan

"Identity is a prison you can never escape, but the way to redeem your past is not to run from it, but to try to understand it, and use it as a foundation to grow." — Jay-Z

"There are no mistakes, only opportunities."

—Tina Fey

"It takes 20 years to build a reputation and five minutes to ruin it. If you think about that, you'll do things differently."
—Warren Buffett

"As you grow older, you will discover that you have two hands, one for helping yourself, the other for helping others."
—Audrey Hepburn

"Sometimes you can't see yourself clearly until you see yourself through the eyes of others."
—Ellen DeGeneres

"You must not lose faith in humanity. Humanity is an ocean; if a few drops of the ocean are dirty, the ocean does not become dirty."
—Mahatma Gandhi

"All life is an experiment. The more experiments you make, the better." –Ralph Waldo Emerson

"Here's to the crazy ones, the misfits, the rebels, the troublemakers, the round pegs in the square holes ... the ones who see things differently — they're not fond of rules ... You can quote them, disagree with them, glorify or vilify them, but the only thing you can't do is ignore them because they change things ... They push the human race forward, and while some may see them as the crazy ones, we see genius ..."

– Steve Jobs

"It had long since come to my attention that people of accomplishment rarely sat back and let things happen to them. They went out and happened to things."

– Leonardo Da Vinci

"Throughout life people
will make you mad,
disrespect you and
treat you bad. Let God
deal with the things
they do, cause hate in
your heart will consume
you too."
— Will Smith

"Do not dwell in the past, do not dream of the future, concentrate the mind on the present moment."

– *Buddha*

"Life is a dream for the wise, a game for the fool, a comedy for the rich, a tragedy for the poor."

– Sholom Aleichem

"If you love life, don't waste time, for time is what life is made up of."

– Bruce Lee

When one door closes, another opens; but we often look so long and so regretfully upon the closed door that we do not see the one that has opened for us.

– Alexander Graham Bell

"Never take life seriously.
Nobody gets out alive
anyway."

— Anonymous

"Be happy for this moment. This moment is your life."

– Omar Khayyam

"Happiness is the feeling that power increases — that resistance is being overcome."
— Friedrich Nietzsche

"I have learned to seek my happiness by limiting my desires, rather than in attempting to satisfy them."
— John Stuart Mill

"The secret of happiness, you see is not found in seeking more, but in developing the capacity to enjoy less."
— **Socrates**

"The more man mediates upon good thoughts, the better will be his world and the world at large."
— Confucius

"The greatest blessings of mankind are within us and within our reach. A wise man is content with his lot, whatever it may be, without wishing for what he has not."
— Seneca

"Happiness is like a butterfly; the more you chase it, the more it will elude you, but if you turn your attention to other things, it will come and sit softly on your shoulder."

— Henry David Thoreau

"When it is obvious that goals can't be reached, don't adjust the goals, but adjust the action steps."
— Confucius

"There may be people who have more talent than you, but there's no excuse for anyone to work harder than you do and I believe that."
— Derek Jeter

"Don't be afraid to fail. It's not the end of the world, and in many ways, it's the first step toward learning something and getting better at it."

— Jon Hamm

"The minute that you're not learning I believe you're dead."
– Jack Nicholson

"Life's tough, but it's tougher when you're stupid."
– John Wayne

"I think if you live in a black and white world, you're going to suffer a lot. I used to be like that. But I don't believe that anymore."
– Bradley Cooper

"I don't believe in happy endings, but I do believe in happy travels, because ultimately, you die at a very young age, or you live long enough to watch your friends die. It's a mean thing, life."

– George Clooney

"It's never too late –
never too late to start
over, never too late to
be happy."
– Jane Fonda

"You're only human. You live once and life is wonderful, so eat the damned red velvet cupcake."
– Emma Stone

"A lot of people give up just before they're about to make it. You know you never know when that next obstacle is going to be the last one."
– Chuck Norris

"Be nice to people on the way up, because you may meet them on the way down."
– Jimmy Durante

"I believe you make your day. You make your life. So much of it is all perception, and this is the form that I built for myself. I have to accept it and work within those compounds, and it's up to me." – **Brad Pitt**

"Life is very interesting... in the end, some of your greatest pains, become your greatest strengths."

– Drew Barrymore